STATE PROFILES

MICHIGAN

BY BETSY RATHBURN

BLASTOFF! DISCOVERY

BELLWETHER MEDIA • MINNEAPOLIS, MN

Blastoff! Discovery launches a new mission: reading to learn. Filled with facts and features, each book offers you an exciting new world to explore!

This edition first published in 2022 by Bellwether Media, Inc.

No part of this publication may be reproduced in whole or in part without written permission of the publisher.
For information regarding permission, write to Bellwether Media, Inc.,
Attention: Permissions Department,
6012 Blue Circle Drive, Minnetonka, MN 55343.

Library of Congress Cataloging-in-Publication Data

Names: Rathburn, Betsy, author.
Title: Michigan / by Betsy Rathburn.
Description: Minneapolis, MN : Bellwether Media, Inc., 2022. |
   Series: Blastoff! Discovery: State profiles | Includes bibliographical
   references and index. | Audience: Ages 7-13 | Audience: Grades
   4-6 | Summary: "Engaging images accompany information
   about Michigan. The combination of high-interest subject matter and
   narrative text is intended for students in grades 3 through 8"
   – Provided by publisher.
Identifiers: LCCN 2021019637 (print) | LCCN 2021019638 (ebook)
   | ISBN 9781644873939 (library binding) |
   ISBN 9781648341700 (ebook)
Subjects: LCSH: Michigan–Juvenile literature.
Classification: LCC F566.3 .R37 2022 (print) | LCC F566.3 (ebook)
   | DDC 977.4–dc23
LC record available at https://lccn.loc.gov/2021019637
LC ebook record available at https://lccn.loc.gov/2021019638

Editor: Colleen Sexton   Designer: Laura Sowers

Printed in the United States of America, North Mankato, MN.

TABLE OF CONTENTS

Sleeping Bear Dunes	4
Where Is Michigan?	6
Michigan's Beginnings	8
Landscape and Climate	10
Wildlife	12
People and Communities	14
Detroit	16
Industry	18
Food	20
Sports and Entertainment	22
Festivals and Traditions	24
Michigan Timeline	26
Michigan Facts	28
Glossary	30
To Learn More	31
Index	32

Time to climb! A family is on vacation at Sleeping Bear **Dunes** National Lakeshore. They head to one of its most famous attractions, a dune that stands 110 feet (33.5 meters) tall. The Dune Climb is tough, but the family makes it to the top. Below, Glen Lake sparkles in the sun.

4

A GREAT NAME

Michigan is known as the Great Lakes State. Four of the five Great Lakes border Michigan. Lakes Superior, Michigan, Huron, and Erie carved out its shores.

DETROIT INSTITUTE OF ARTS

HENRY FORD MUSEUM OF AMERICAN INNOVATION

MACKINAC ISLAND

TAHQUAMENON FALLS

The next day, the family hikes to Pyramid Point. The top of this high **bluff** offers amazing views of Lake Michigan. The family ends the day at the beach. The lake's cool water feels good under the summer sun. Welcome to Michigan!

5

Michigan is in the **Upper Midwest**. The state covers 96,714 square miles (250,488 square kilometers). Michigan has two parts. The Lower **Peninsula** lies between Lake Michigan to the west and Lake Huron to the east. Lake Erie and Canada meet the southeastern border. Ohio and Indiana are neighbors to the south. The capital, Lansing, is in the Lower Peninsula. Other major cities there include Detroit, Grand Rapids, and Ann Arbor.

The Upper Peninsula sits between Lake Superior to the north and Lake Michigan to the south. Wisconsin lies to the southwest, and Canada reaches the northeastern border. The Upper Peninsula's largest city is Marquette.

ISLE ROYALE

WISCONSIN

ILLINOIS

N
W + E
S

LAKE
SUPERIOR

ISLE ROYALE

Isle Royale lies north of the
Upper Peninsula in Lake Superior.
Although it is closer to Canada
and Minnesota, the island is part
of Michigan. The entire island is a
national park!

MARQUETTE

CANADA

UPPER PENINSULA

LAKE
HURON

LAKE
MICHIGAN

MICHIGAN

LOWER PENINSULA

GRAND RAPIDS

 LANSING

CANADA

ANN ARBOR

DETROIT

INDIANA

OHIO

LAKE
ERIE

DETROIT, 1815

The first people arrived in Michigan thousands of years ago. They used long spears to hunt large animals. Later, the Ottawa, Chippewa, Miami, Potawatomi, and Wyandot groups formed. These Native Americans hunted, fished, and grew crops. They traveled the Great Lakes in long canoes.

In the 1600s, European **settlers** arrived in Michigan. Many were fur traders and **missionaries**. Most French settlers befriended the area's Native Americans. But British settlers did not. The British fought the French and Native Americans to take control of Michigan. After the **Revolutionary War**, the United States gained control of Michigan. It became the 26th state in 1837.

NATIVE PEOPLES OF MICHIGAN

CHIPPEWA INDIANS

- Original lands in Michigan's Upper Peninsula and eastern Lower Peninsula
- Around 44,000 in Michigan today
- Also called Ojibwe and Anishinaabe

OTTAWA INDIANS

- Original lands in Michigan's western Lower Peninsula
- Around 850 on three reservations in Michigan today
- Also called Odawa

POTAWATOMI INDIANS

- Original lands in southwestern Michigan
- Around 800 on four reservations in Michigan today
- Also called Neshnabé

Michigan's Lower Peninsula is part of the Central Lowland region. It is mostly flat. Many farms spread across this area. Bluffs and sand dunes line the coast. Lowlands in the eastern Upper Peninsula include many swamps. The Upper Peninsula slopes up to rugged hills in the west. The Porcupine and Huron Mountains rise in this area. Forests cover much of the Upper Peninsula.

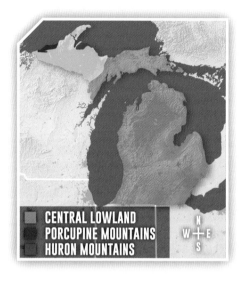

CENTRAL LOWLAND
PORCUPINE MOUNTAINS
HURON MOUNTAINS

N
W+E
S

PORCUPINE MOUNTAINS

LAKE MICHIGAN COAST

SPRING
HIGH: 54°F (12°C)
LOW: 33°F (1°C)

SUMMER
HIGH: 78°F (26°C)
LOW: 56°F (13°C)

FALL
HIGH: 57°F (14°C)
LOW: 39°F (4°C)

WINTER
HIGH: 30°F (-1°C)
LOW: 15°F (-9°C)

°F = degrees Fahrenheit
°C = degrees Celsius

MICHIGAN'S CHALLENGE: CLIMATE CHANGE

Climate change is leading to more rainfall and increased flooding in Michigan. Flooding damages crops. It may also cause chemicals to enter lakes and rivers. That could make water supplies unsafe to drink.

Michigan has warm summers and cold winters. Temperatures are usually cooler in the Upper Peninsula. **Lake effect** snowstorms affect western Michigan and the Upper Peninsula. These storms can dump many inches of snow at one time!

11

Michigan's forests are home to many animals. Squirrels and chipmunks scurry along tree branches. White-tailed deer munch on leaves and twigs. Black bears and coyotes track them through the trees. Gray wolves hunt in packs at night. Raccoons and opossums also explore forests at night.

Near ponds, bullfrogs croak while painted turtles sun themselves. Walleye and trout swim in Michigan's lakes and rivers. Cardinals, owls, and woodpeckers fly through meadows and woodlands. American robins peck the ground for worms. The trumpeting sound of sandhill cranes announces their arrival each spring. Canada geese also **migrate** through the state.

RACCOON

SANDHILL CRANE

BROOK TROUT

BLACK BEAR

AMERICAN BULLFROG

GRAY WOLF

Life Span: up to 13 years
Status: least concern

gray wolf range = █

LEAST CONCERN	NEAR THREATENED	VULNERABLE	ENDANGERED	CRITICALLY ENDANGERED	EXTINCT IN THE WILD	EXTINCT

13

PEOPLE AND COMMUNITIES

More than 10 million people live in Michigan. About three in four Michiganders live in **urban** areas. Most of the state's cities lie in the Lower Peninsula. **Rural** residents live on farms and in small towns.

ANOTHER NAME

Michigan's Upper Peninsula is often called the U.P. People who live there are called Yoopers!

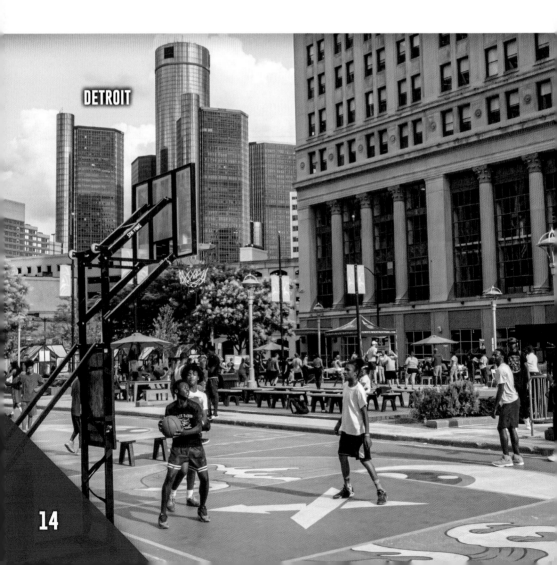

DETROIT

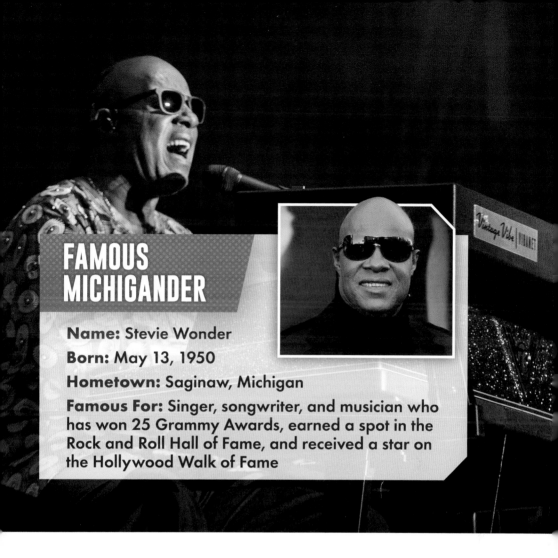

FAMOUS MICHIGANDER

Name: Stevie Wonder
Born: May 13, 1950
Hometown: Saginaw, Michigan
Famous For: Singer, songwriter, and musician who has won 25 Grammy Awards, earned a spot in the Rock and Roll Hall of Fame, and received a star on the Hollywood Walk of Fame

About three out of four Michiganders have **ancestors** from Germany, Ireland, the Netherlands, and other European countries. The next-largest groups are Black or African Americans and Hispanic Americans. Smaller numbers have Asian or Native American backgrounds. Most Native Americans live in cities, but some make their homes on the state's 12 **reservations**. Michigan welcomes many **immigrants**. Most come from Mexico, India, Iraq, China, and Canada.

Detroit is Michigan's largest city. It sits in the southeast on a bend in the Detroit River. Founded in 1701, Detroit became a **manufacturing** center. Today, Detroit is known as Motor City. It is the center of the country's automobile industry. Large automakers based there employ thousands of workers in their factories.

Detroit is a **cultural** center. Visitors enjoy paintings and sculptures at the Detroit Institute of Arts. The Charles H. Wright Museum holds the world's largest African American history exhibit. The Motown Museum explores Detroit's musical history. Shoppers head to the huge Eastern Market to buy food and browse goods from local artists.

MOTOWN MUSEUM

A MUSICAL CITY

Detroit is famous for a rhythm and blues style of music called Motown. Motown has been popular since the 1960s. It gets its name from a Detroit record company that released many hit songs in this style.

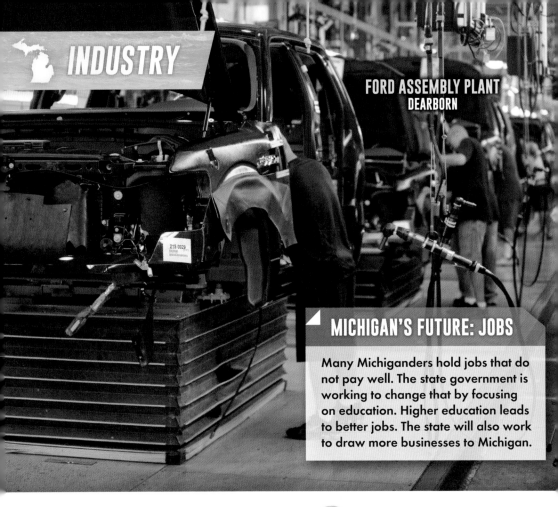

INDUSTRY

FORD ASSEMBLY PLANT
DEARBORN

MICHIGAN'S FUTURE: JOBS

Many Michiganders hold jobs that do not pay well. The state government is working to change that by focusing on education. Higher education leads to better jobs. The state will also work to draw more businesses to Michigan.

Michigan's early economy centered on fur trading and lumber. By the late 1800s, factories were turning out railroad cars, stoves, and other metal items. Today, manufacturing is still one of Michigan's top industries. Factory workers make car parts, chemicals, and food products.

IT'S A BOWL!

The cereal-maker Kellogg's is based in Battle Creek. The city became known as the Cereal Bowl of America!

Top farm crops in Michigan include soybeans and corn. Fruit growers produce blueberries, cherries, and apples. Livestock farmers raise dairy cows, beef cattle, and hogs. Mining is important, too. Miners drill for oil in the Lower Peninsula and dig up iron ore in the Upper Peninsula. Most Michiganders hold **service jobs**. They work in hospitals, schools, and government offices.

INVENTED IN MICHIGAN

MOVING ASSEMBLY LINE
Date Invented: 1913
Inventor: Henry Ford

THREE-COLORED TRAFFIC SIGNAL
Date Invented: 1920
Inventor: William Potts

PAINT-BY-NUMBER KITS
Date Invented: 1949
Inventor: Dan Robbins

CENTERLINE ROAD MARKINGS
Date Invented: 1911
Inventor: Edward N. Hines

CHICKEN SHAWARMA

Michiganders have many favorite foods. Shawarma is popular in Detroit. Cooks thinly slice this flavorful roast meat and stuff it into pita bread along with vegetables. Detroit-style pizza is known for its rectangular shape. Meat-filled pastry pockets called pasties appear on menus in the Upper Peninsula. Coney dogs are a Michigan classic. Chili, cheese, and onions top these hot dogs.

Michiganders enjoy sweet treats. Mackinac Island is famous for its fudge. Popular flavors include chocolate, mint, and peanut butter. Bakers make Polish doughnuts called *paczki* filled with jelly and covered in powdered sugar or icing. Hot apple cider and cider doughnuts are fall favorites.

MACKINAC ISLAND FUDGE

PACZKI

PASTIES

Ask an adult to help you make this recipe.

6
SERVINGS

FILLING INGREDIENTS

2 cups diced potatoes
1 large onion, diced
1 cup diced rutabaga
1/2 cup diced carrot
1 1/2 teaspoons salt
1/2 teaspoon pepper
1 1/2 pounds ground lean beef, cooked and drained

CRUST INGREDIENTS

6 cups flour
1 tablespoon salt
1 pound shortening (2 1/3 cups)

DIRECTIONS

1. In a large bowl, mix all filling ingredients and set aside.

2. In a medium bowl, mix the flour and salt. Then cut in the shortening until crumbly.

3. Divide the dough into 6 equal rounds and roll out flat. Place one-sixth of the filling in the middle of each crust. Fold over the crust and crimp the edges.

4. Place the pasties on an ungreased cookie sheet and bake at 350 degrees Fahrenheit (177 degrees Celsius) for about 75 minutes. Serve warm.

In summer, Michiganders like to get outdoors. They pitch tents and hike trails in state parks. Kayakers explore sea caves along the Lake Superior shoreline. Michigan's lakes are popular fishing spots. Sightseers visit hundreds of waterfalls in the Upper Peninsula. In winter, skiers and snowboarders head to the Porcupine Mountains. Year-round, Michigan's cities draw visitors for concerts, theater performances, and museum exhibits.

Michigan's sports fans cheer on professional baseball, basketball, football, and hockey teams. College football is wildly popular. Every fall, crowds fill the stands to watch players from the University of Michigan and Michigan State University take the field.

FOOTBALL FEUD

Every year, the University of Michigan Wolverines play against the Ohio State Buckeyes. Millions tune in to watch the game. It is one of the biggest rivalries in college football!

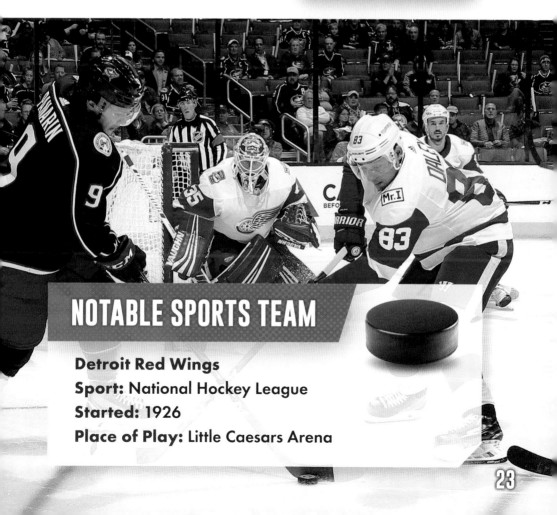

NOTABLE SPORTS TEAM

Detroit Red Wings
Sport: National Hockey League
Started: 1926
Place of Play: Little Caesars Arena

LITTLE RIVER BAND OF
OTTAWA INDIANS POWWOW

Michiganders honor their differences. The American Polish Festival in Sterling Heights celebrates Polish culture with polka music and dancing. Detroit's African World Festival features music, art, fashion shows, and **traditional** foods. Michiganders gather at Native American **powwows** throughout the state. They enjoy traditional songs, dances, foods, and crafts.

Detroit hosts the North American International Auto Show. Every year, automakers from around the world show off their latest models. At the Ann Arbor Art Fair, thousands of artists display and sell their work. The Michigan Tech Winter Carnival features snow sculptures, sleigh rides, and outdoor games. Michigan is full of fun!

FRANKENMUTH

Visitors to the town of Frankenmuth might feel like they are in Germany. The buildings reflect the style of buildings in Bavaria, a part of southern Germany. The town is even known as Little Bavaria!

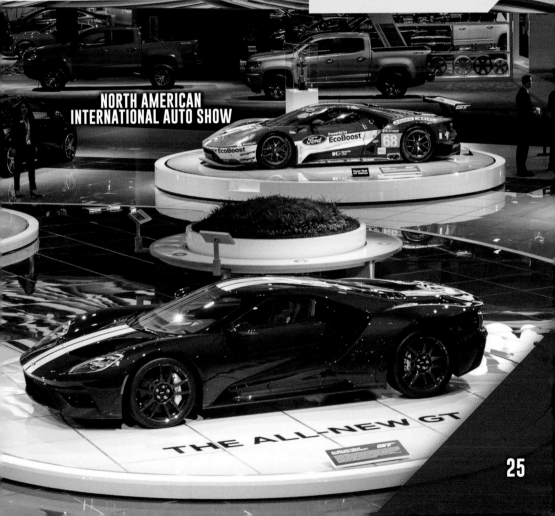

NORTH AMERICAN INTERNATIONAL AUTO SHOW

THE ALL-NEW GT

1783
The United States gains control of Michigan

1825
The Erie Canal in New York is completed, making it easier for settlers to travel to Michigan

1622
Étienne Brulé is the first European to visit Michigan

1837
Michigan becomes the 26th state

1668
Sault Sainte Marie is founded, becoming the oldest European settlement in Michigan

1840s
The discovery of iron and copper brings settlers to the Upper Peninsula

1847

Michigan's capital moves
from Detroit to Lansing

1967

Poverty and racism
in Detroit spark riots

1903

The Ford Motor Company
is founded in Detroit

2015

The city of Flint comes under
a state of emergency when
high levels of lead are found
in its water supply

Nicknames: The Great Lakes State, The Wolverine State, The Mitten State

Motto: *Si Quaeris Peninsulam Amoenam, Circumspice* (If You Seek a Pleasant Peninsula, Look About You).

Date of Statehood: January 26, 1837 (the 26th state)

Capital City: Lansing ★

Other Major Cities: Detroit, Grand Rapids, Warren, Sterling Heights, Ann Arbor, Marquette

Area: 96,714 square miles (250,488 square kilometers); Michigan is the 11th largest state.

Population
10,077,331
(2020)

STATE FLAG

Adopted in 1911, Michigan's dark blue flag features the state's coat of arms. An elk and a moose stand on either side of a shield. A man on the shield walks next to a lake as the sun rises. A bald eagle perched above the shield holds an olive branch and arrows. Michigan's state motto lies below the shield.

INDUSTRY

Main Exports

motor vehicles and parts

computer parts

chemicals

natural gas

aircraft

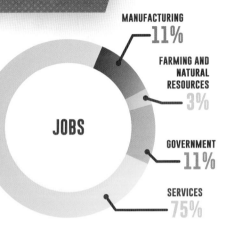

JOBS

MANUFACTURING
11%

FARMING AND NATURAL RESOURCES
3%

GOVERNMENT
11%

SERVICES
75%

Natural Resources
timber, iron ore, copper, natural gas, salt, sand, gravel

GOVERNMENT

15 ELECTORAL VOTES

Federal Government
13 REPRESENTATIVES | **2** SENATORS

USA

MI

State Government
110 REPRESENTATIVES | **38** SENATORS

STATE SYMBOLS

STATE BIRD
AMERICAN ROBIN

STATE FISH
BROOK TROUT

STATE FLOWER
APPLE BLOSSOM

STATE TREE
EASTERN WHITE PINE

GLOSSARY

ancestors—relatives who lived long ago

bluff—a cliff or steep bank that often overlooks a body of water

cultural—relating to the beliefs, arts, and ways of life in a place or society

dunes—hills of sand

immigrants—people who move to a new country

lake effect—a weather condition in which warm, wet air rises from a body of water and mixes with cold, dry air above; the lake effect often leads to heavy snowfall.

manufacturing—a field of work in which people use machines to make products

migrate—to travel from one place to another, often with the seasons

missionaries—people sent to a place to spread a religious faith

peninsula—a section of land that extends out from a larger piece of land and is almost completely surrounded by water

powwows—Native American gatherings that usually include dancing

reservations—areas of land that are controlled by Native American tribes

Revolutionary War—the war from 1775 to 1783 in which the United States fought for independence from Great Britain

rural—related to the countryside

service jobs—jobs that perform tasks for people or businesses

settlers—people who move to live in a new, undeveloped region

traditional—related to customs, ideas, or beliefs handed down from one generation to the next

Upper Midwest—a region of the United States that includes Minnesota, Wisconsin, Michigan, Iowa, North Dakota, and South Dakota

urban—related to cities and city life

TO LEARN MORE

AT THE LIBRARY

Gregory, Josh. *Michigan*. New York, N.Y.: Children's Press, 2018.

Knutson, Julie. *Flint Water Crisis*. Ann Arbor, Mich.: Cherry Lake Publishing, 2021.

Ryan, Todd. *Michigan Wolverines*. Minneapolis, Minn.: Abdo Publishing, 2020.

ON THE WEB

FACTSURFER

Factsurfer.com gives you a safe, fun way to find more information.

1. Go to www.factsurfer.com.

2. Enter "Michigan" into the search box and click 🔍.

3. Select your book cover to see a list of related content.

INDEX

African World Festival, 24

American Polish Festival, 24

Ann Arbor Art Fair, 25

arts, 17, 22, 24, 25

capital (see Lansing)

challenge, 11

climate, 11

Detroit, 6, 7, 8, 14, 16–17, 20, 24, 25

Detroit Red Wings, 23

fast facts, 28–29

festivals, 24–25

food, 20–21

future, 18

history, 8–9, 16, 17, 18

inventions, 19

Isle Royale, 6, 7

Lake Erie, 5, 6, 7

Lake Huron, 5, 6, 7

Lake Michigan, 5, 6, 7, 11

Lake Superior, 5, 6, 7, 22

landmarks, 4, 5, 7, 17, 21, 25

landscape, 4, 5, 10–11, 12, 16, 22

Lansing, 6, 7

location, 6–7

Lower Peninsula, 6, 7, 10, 14, 19

Marquette, 6, 7

Michigan Tech Winter Carnival, 25

Motown, 17

North American International Auto Show, 25

outdoor activities, 4, 5, 22, 25

people, 8, 9, 14–15, 24

Porcupine Mountains, 10, 22

recipe, 21

Revolutionary War, 9

size, 6

Sleeping Bear Dunes National Lakeshore, 4–5

sports, 23

timeline, 26–27

Upper Peninsula, 6, 7, 10, 11, 14, 19, 20, 22

wildlife, 12–13

Wonder, Stevie, 15

working, 16, 18–19

The images in this book are reproduced through the courtesy of: Lonnie Paulson, front cover, pp. 2-3; Gestalt Imagery, p. 3; Sally Weigand/ Alamy, pp. 4-5; Susan Montgomery, p. 5 (Makinac Island); Kenneth Keifer, p. 5 (Tahquamenon Falls); David R. Frazier Photolibrary, Inc./ Alamy, p. 5 (Detroit Institute of Arts); Aldo91, p. 5 (Henry Ford Museum); North Wind Picture Archives/ Alamy, p. 8; ehrlif, pp. 9, 11; PQK, p. 10; John McCormick, p. 11 (temperature inset); Jiang Honyan, p. 12 (bullfrog); Paul Reeves Photography, p. 12 (raccoon); Brian Lasenby, p. 12 (sandhill crane); Rostislav Stefanek, pp. 12 (trout), 29 (trout); Gagat55, p. 12 (black bear); Holly Kuchera, p. 13; Paolo Novello, p. 14; Kobby Dagan, p. 15 (Stevie Wonder background); Tinseltown, p. 15 (Stevie Wonder inset); f11photo, p. 16; Fotografia Inc., p. 17; Spencer Grant/ Art Directors/ Alamy, p. 18; Andre Jenny/ Alamy, p. 18 (Kellogg's); matthew siddons, p. 19; Wikipedia, p. 19 (assembly line); krolya25, p. 19 (paint); andregric, p. 19 (paintbrush); Odua Images, p. 19 (traffic light); MintImages, p. 19 (centerline); Irina Burakova, p. 20; Danita Delimont/ Alamy, p. 21 (fudge); Brent Hofacker, p. 21 (paczki, pasties background); Richard Griffin, p. 21 (pasties); genesisgraphics, p. 22; Cal Sport Media/ Alamy, p. 23 (football feud); Tribune Content Agency LLC/ Alamy, p. 23 (Detroit Red Wings); aperturesound, p. 23 (puck); Darlene Stanley, p. 24; Alexander Sviridov, p. 25 (Frankenmuth); Steve Lagreca, p. 25 (North American International Auto Show); Craig Sterken, pp. 26-32; Everett Collection, p. 26 (Erie Canal); Sueddeutsche Zeitung Photo/ Alamy, p. 27 (Ford Motor Company); ccool/ Alamy, p. 27 (Detroit riots); Reuters/ Alamy, p. 27 (Flint water crisis); Millenius, p. 28; Jeff Rzepka, p. 29 (robin); Fedorov Oleksiy, p. 29 (apple blossom); Pam Carnell, p. 29 (eastern white pine); Billion Photos, p. 31.